This journal belongs to

belongs

to

_____

My Expense Log

Date	Item(s)	Store	Cost

My Expense Log

Date	Item(s)	Store	Cost

WEEKLY

Monday	Tuesday	Wednes day	Thursday

NOTES

Friday	Saturday	Sunday

My Expense Log

Date	Item(s)	Store	Cost

My Expense Log

Date	Item(s)	Store	Cost

WEEKLY

Monday	Tuesday	Wednes day	Thursday

NOTES

Friday	Saturday	Sunday

My Expense Log

Date	Item(s)	Store	Cost

My Expense Log

Date	Item(s)	Store	Cost

WEEKLY

Monday	Tuesday	Wednes day	Thursday

NOTES

Friday	Saturday	Sunday

My Expense Log

Date	Item(s)	Store	Cost

My Expense Log

Date	Item(s)	Store	Cost

WEEKLY

Monday	Tuesday	Wednesday	Thursday

NOTES

Friday	Saturday	Sunday

My Expense Log

Date	Item(s)	Store	Cost

My Expense Log

Date	Item(s)	Store	Cost

WEEKLY

Monday	Tuesday	Wednesday	Thursday

NOTES

Friday	Saturday	Sunday

My Expense Log

Date	Item(s)	Store	Cost

My Expense Log

Date	Item(s)	Store	Cost

WEEKLY

Monday	Tuesday	Wednesday	Thursday

NOTES

Friday	Saturday	Sunday

My Expense Log

Date	Item(s)	Store	Cost

My Expense Log

Date	Item(s)	Store	Cost

WEEKLY

Monday	Tuesday	Wednes day	Thursday

NOTES

Friday	Saturday	Sunday

My Expense Log

Date	Item(s)	Store	Cost

My Expense Log

Date	Item(s)	Store	Cost

WEEKLY

Monday	Tuesday	Wednesday	Thursday

NOTES

Friday	Saturday	Sunday

My Expense Log

Date	Item(s)	Store	Cost

My Expense Log

Date	Item(s)	Store	Cost

WEEKLY

Monday	Tuesday	Wednes day	Thursday

NOTES

Friday	Saturday	Sunday

My Expense Log

Date	Item(s)	Store	Cost

My Expense Log

Date	Item(s)	Store	Cost

WEEKLY

Monday	Tuesday	Wednes day	Thursday

NOTES

Friday	Saturday	Sunday

My Expense Log

Date	Item(s)	Store	Cost

My Expense Log

Date	Item(s)	Store	Cost

WEEKLY

Monday	Tuesday	Wednesday	Thursday

NOTES

Friday	Saturday	Sunday

My Expense Log

Date	Item(s)	Store	Cost

My Expense Log

Date	Item(s)	Store	Cost

WEEKLY

Monday	Tuesday	Wednes day	Thursday

NOTES

Friday	Saturday	Sunday

My Expense Log

Date	Item(s)	Store	Cost

My Expense Log

Date	Item(s)	Store	Cost

WEEKLY

Monday	Tuesday	Wednesday	Thursday

NOTES

Friday	Saturday	Sunday

My Expense Log

Date	Item(s)	Store	Cost

My Expense Log

Date	Item(s)	Store	Cost

WEEKLY

Monday	Tuesday	Wednes day	Thursday

NOTES

Friday	Saturday	Sunday

My Expense Log

Date	Item(s)	Store	Cost

My Expense Log

Date	Item(s)	Store	Cost

WEEKLY

Monday	Tuesday	Wednesday	Thursday

NOTES

Friday	Saturday	Sunday

My Expense Log

Date	Item(s)	Store	Cost

My Expense Log

Date	Item(s)	Store	Cost

WEEKLY

Monday	Tuesday	Wednes day	Thursday

NOTES

Friday	Saturday	Sunday

My Expense Log

Date	Item(s)	Store	Cost

My Expense Log

Date	Item(s)	Store	Cost

WEEKLY

Monday	Tuesday	Wednes day	Thursday

NOTES

Friday	Saturday	Sunday

My Expense Log

Date	Item(s)	Store	Cost

My Expense Log

Date	Item(s)	Store	Cost

WEEKLY

Monday	Tuesday	Wednes day	Thursday

NOTES

Friday	Saturday	Sunday

My Expense Log

Date	Item(s)	Store	Cost

My Expense Log

Date	Item(s)	Store	Cost

WEEKLY

Monday	Tuesday	Wednes day	Thursday

NOTES

Friday	Saturday	Sunday

My Expense Log

Date	Item(s)	Store	Cost

My Expense Log

Date	Item(s)	Store	Cost

WEEKLY

Monday	Tuesday	Wednes day	Thursday

NOTES

Friday	Saturday	Sunday

My Expense Log

Date	Item(s)	Store	Cost

My Expense Log

Date	Item(s)	Store	Cost

WEEKLY

Monday	Tuesday	Wednesday	Thursday

NOTES

Friday	Saturday	Sunday

My Expense Log

Date	Item(s)	Store	Cost

My Expense Log

Date	Item(s)	Store	Cost

WEEKLY

Monday	Tuesday	Wednes day	Thursday

NOTES

Friday	Saturday	Sunday

My Expense Log

Date	Item(s)	Store	Cost

My Expense Log

Date	Item(s)	Store	Cost

WEEKLY

Monday	Tuesday	Wednes day	Thursday

NOTES

Friday	Saturday	Sunday

My Expense Log

Date	Item(s)	Store	Cost

My Expense Log

Date	Item(s)	Store	Cost

WEEKLY

Monday	Tuesday	Wednes day	Thursday

NOTES

Friday	Saturday	Sunday

My Expense Log

Date	Item(s)	Store	Cost

My Expense Log

Date	Item(s)	Store	Cost

WEEKLY

Monday	Tuesday	Wednes day	Thursday

NOTES

Friday	Saturday	Sunday

My Expense Log

Date	Item(s)	Store	Cost

My Expense Log

Date	Item(s)	Store	Cost

WEEKLY

Monday	Tuesday	Wednes day	Thursday

NOTES

Friday	Saturday	Sunday

My Expense Log

Date	Item(s)	Store	Cost

My Expense Log

Date	Item(s)	Store	Cost

WEEKLY

Monday	Tuesday	Wednes day	Thursday

NOTES

Friday	Saturday	Sunday

My Expense Log

Date	Item(s)	Store	Cost

My Expense Log

Date	Item(s)	Store	Cost

WEEKLY

Monday	Tuesday	Wednes day	Thursday

NOTES

Friday	Saturday	Sunday

My Expense Log

Date	Item(s)	Store	Cost

My Expense Log

Date	Item(s)	Store	Cost

WEEKLY

Monday	Tuesday	Wednes day	Thursday

NOTES

Friday	Saturday	Sunday

My Expense Log

Date	Item(s)	Store	Cost

My Expense Log

Date	Item(s)	Store	Cost

WEEKLY

Monday	Tuesday	Wednes day	Thursday

NOTES

Friday	Saturday	Sunday

My Expense Log

Date	Item(s)	Store	Cost

My Expense Log

Date	Item(s)	Store	Cost

WEEKLY

Monday	Tuesday	Wednes day	Thursday

NOTES

Friday	Saturday	Sunday

My Expense Log

Date	Item(s)	Store	Cost

My Expense Log

Date	Item(s)	Store	Cost

WEEKLY

Monday	Tuesday	Wednes day	Thursday

NOTES

Friday	Saturday	Sunday

My Expense Log

Date	Item(s)	Store	Cost

My Expense Log

Date	Item(s)	Store	Cost

WEEKLY

Monday	Tuesday	Wednes day	Thursday

NOTES

Friday	Saturday	Sunday

My Expense Log

Date	Item(s)	Store	Cost

My Expense Log

Date	Item(s)	Store	Cost

WEEKLY

Monday	Tuesday	Wednes day	Thursday

NOTES

Friday	Saturday	Sunday

My Expense Log

Date	Item(s)	Store	Cost

My Expense Log

Date	Item(s)	Store	Cost

WEEKLY

Monday	Tuesday	Wednes day	Thursday

NOTES

Friday	Saturday	Sunday

My Expense Log

Date	Item(s)	Store	Cost

My Expense Log

Date	Item(s)	Store	Cost

WEEKLY

Monday	Tuesday	Wednes day	Thursday

NOTES

Friday	Saturday	Sunday